HERE'S WHERE HISTORY HAPPENED!

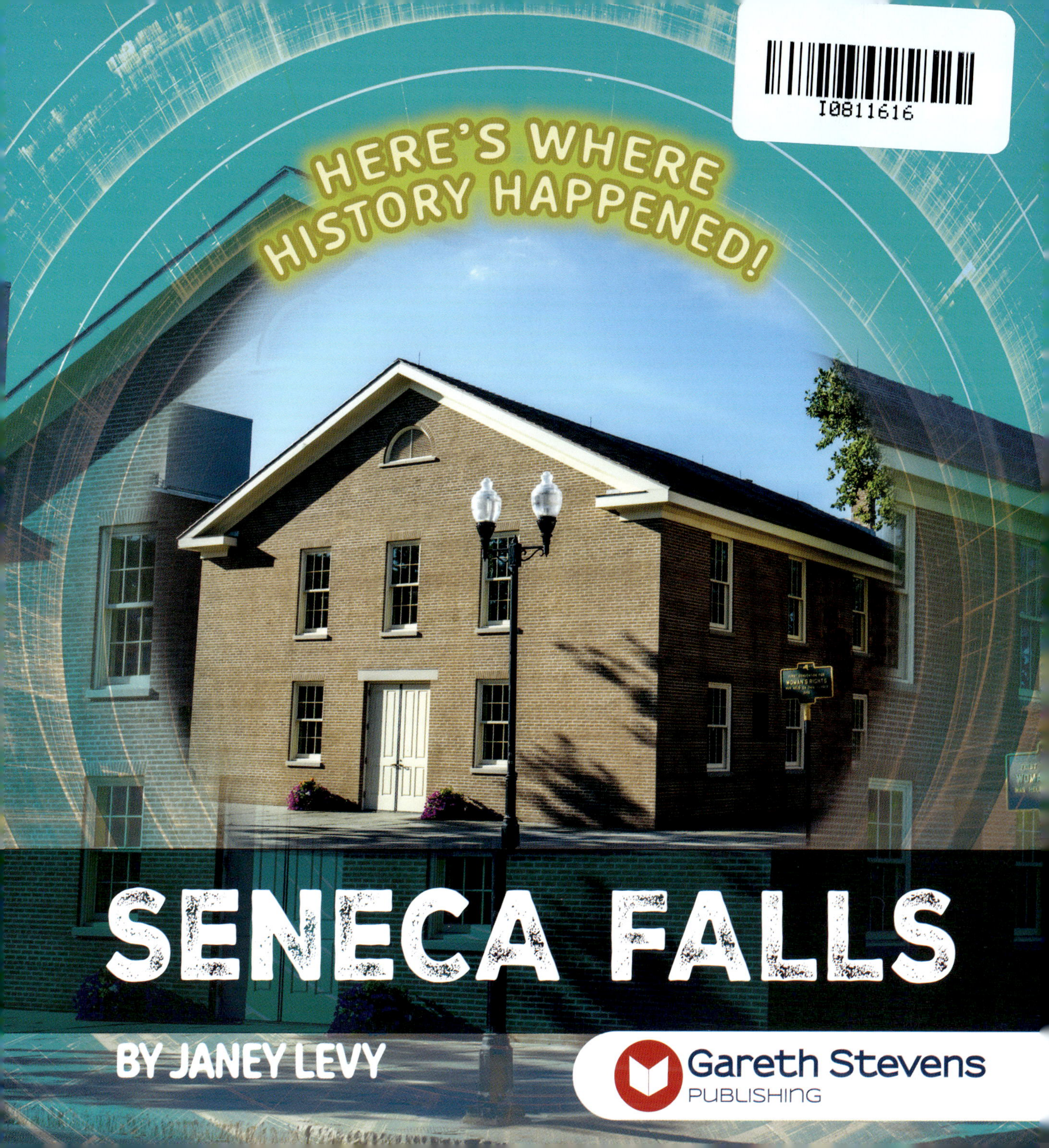

SENECA FALLS

BY JANEY LEVY

Gareth Stevens PUBLISHING

Please visit our website, www.garethstevens.com. For a free color catalog of all our high-quality books, call toll free 1-800-542-2595 or fax 1-877-542-2596.

Library of Congress Cataloging-in-Publication Data
Names: Levy, Janey, author.
Title: Seneca Falls / Janey Levy.
Description: [Buffalo] : Gareth Stevens Publishing, [2025] | Series: Here's where history happened! | Includes bibliographical references and index. | Audience: Grades 2-3
Identifiers: LCCN 2023053519 (print) | LCCN 2023053520 (ebook) | ISBN 9781482466447 (library binding) | ISBN 9781482466430 (paperback) | ISBN 9781482466454 (ebook)
Subjects: LCSH: Woman's Rights Convention (1848 : Seneca Falls, N.Y.)–Juvenile literature. | Women's rights–New York (State)–Seneca Falls–History–Juvenile literature. | Women–Suffrage–United States–History–Juvenile literature. | Feminism–United States–History–19th century–Juvenile literature.
Classification: LCC HQ1418 .L48 2025 (print) | LCC HQ1418 (ebook) | DDC 305.4209747/69–dc23/eng/20231201
LC record available at https://lccn.loc.gov/2023053519
LC ebook record available at https://lccn.loc.gov/2023053520

Published in 2025 by
Gareth Stevens Publishing
2544 Clinton Street
Buffalo, NY 14224

Designer: Tanya Dellaccio Keeney
Editor: Theresa Emminizer

Photo credits: Series background pixelparticle/Shutterstock.com; Cover, p. 5 (building and sign) Alizada Studios/Shutterstock.com; p. 5 (map) Peter Hermes Furian/Shutterstock.com; p. 7 https://upload.wikimedia.org/wikipedia/commons/f/f9/The_Anti-Slavery_Society_Convention%2C_1840_by_Benjamin_Robert_Haydon.jpg; p. 9 https://upload.wikimedia.org/wikipedia/commons/4/48/ElizabethCadyStanton.jpg; p. 11 (Lucretia) https://upload.wikimedia.org/wikipedia/commons/5/57/Mott_Lucretia_Painting_Kyle_1841.jpg; p. 11 (seal) https://upload.wikimedia.org/wikipedia/en/1/12/PFASS_seal.jpg; p. 13 (both) Courtesy of the Library of Congress; p. 15 (Frederick Douglass) pavi8512/Shutterstock.com; p. 15 (Lucretia and James) https://upload.wikimedia.org/wikipedia/commons/b/b4/Lucretia_and_James_Mott.jpg; p. 19 lev radin/Shutterstock.com; p.21 https://upload.wikimedia.org/wikipedia/commons/5/5a/Elizabeth_Cady_Stanton_House_with_plaque_2013.jpg.

Printed in the United States of America

CPSIA compliance information: Batch #CSGS25: For further information contact Gareth Stevens at 1-800-542-2595.

CONTENTS

Words in the glossary appear in **bold** type the first time they are used in the text.

HAVE YOU HEARD OF SENECA FALLS?

Seneca Falls is a small town of about 9,000 people in the middle of New York State. However, when history happened in Seneca Falls in 1848, its population was only about 4,000.

What's so important about Seneca Falls in 1848? The first U.S. women's rights convention, or meeting, was held there that year. Two main organizers, or planners, of the convention were women who had met by chance at another convention in 1840. Keep reading to learn more about the convention and its organizers!

KNOW THE FACTS!

SENECA FALLS WAS HOME TO MANY PEOPLE WHO WANTED TO MAKE SOCIETY BETTER. PEOPLE **SUPPORTED** ABOLITION, OR THE END OF ENSLAVING PEOPLE, AS WELL AS WOMEN'S RIGHTS.

THE WOMEN'S RIGHTS CONVENTION WAS HELD IN THIS SMALL CHURCH, CALLED THE WESLEYAN CHAPEL.

A CHANCE MEETING

The two main organizers of the 1848 convention were Elizabeth Cady Stanton and Lucretia Mott. They happened to meet eight years earlier at the World **Anti-Slavery** Convention in London, England.

Stanton was there with her new husband, who was a **delegate**. Mott was there as a delegate herself. But the convention refused to allow women to take part and forced them to sit in a separate area. Stanton and Mott met in this area and shared their anger over how women were treated.

KNOW THE FACTS!

STANTON AND MOTT FIRST TALKED ABOUT HOLDING A WOMEN'S RIGHTS CONVENTION WHILE THEY WERE AT THE WORLD ANTI-SLAVERY CONVENTION.

THIS IS AN ARTIST'S IDEA OF WHAT THE WORLD ANTI-SLAVERY CONVENTION LOOKED LIKE.

ELIZABETH CADY STANTON

Who was Elizabeth Cady Stanton? She was born Elizabeth Cady on November 12, 1815, in Johnstown, New York. Her father was a **lawyer**, and through him, she learned how few lawful rights women had. This made her angry, and she became set on changing things for women.

In 1840, Elizabeth married Henry B. Stanton, a famous speaker and supporter of abolition. She made her belief in women's rights clear at her wedding. She refused to make the usual promise to obey her husband!

KNOW THE FACTS!

IT WOULD HAVE BEEN USUAL FOR STANTON TO BE CALLED MRS. HENRY B. STANTON AFTER SHE MARRIED. BUT SHE WAS AN INDEPENDENT WOMAN AND CHOSE TO BE KNOWN AS ELIZABETH CADY STANTON!

THIS PICTURE SHOWS ELIZABETH CADY STANTON AS SHE WAS AROUND THE TIME OF THE CONVENTION IN SENECA FALLS.

LUCRETIA MOTT

Lucretia Mott was born Lucretia Coffin on January 3, 1793, in Nantucket, Massachusetts. She was raised in the Quaker faith, which teaches that all people are equal. As a result, Quakers opposed enslaving people. But when Lucretia began teaching in a Quaker school, she discovered women weren't equal. Male teachers earned twice as much!

She married James Mott in 1811. In 1821, she became a Quaker **minister**. She soon began traveling the country giving speeches about peace, abolition, and other issues.

THIS PAINTING OF LUCRETIA MOTT WAS MADE IN 1842, JUST A FEW YEARS BEFORE THE CONVENTION IN SENECA FALLS.

PHILADELPHIA FEMALE ANTI-SLAVERY SOCIETY SEAL

KNOW THE FACTS!

MOTT WAS ONE OF THE FOUNDERS OF THE PHILADELPHIA FEMALE ANTI-SLAVERY SOCIETY IN 1833.

A TEA PARTY STARTS THE ACTION

In 1848, Stanton lived in Seneca Falls, and Mott lived in Philadelphia, Pennsylvania. But Mott was visiting near Seneca Falls. And in early July, they and two other women gathered at their friend Jane Hunt's house for tea.

The women talked about their lives and the problems they faced. Stanton said it was time to talk publicly about how unfairly women were treated and it was up to women to do this. The women agreed to organize a convention.

KNOW THE FACTS!

STANTON, MOTT, AND THE OTHER WOMEN DECIDED TO HOLD THEIR CONVENTION IN SENECA FALLS ON JULY 19 AND 20, 1848—JUST A FEW DAYS AFTER THEY MET FOR TEA!

THE FIRST CONVENTION

EVER CALLED TO DISCUSS THE

Civil and Political Rights of Women,

SENECA FALLS, N. Y., JULY 19, 20, 1848.

WOMAN'S RIGHTS CONVENTION.

A Convention to discuss the social, civil, and religious condition and rights of woman will be held in the Wesleyan Chapel, at Seneca Falls, N. Y., on Wednesday and Thursday, the 19th and 20th of July current; commencing at 10 o'clock A. M. During the first day the meeting will be exclusively for women, who are earnestly invited to attend. The public generally are invited to be present on the second day, when Lucretia Mott, of Philadelphia, and other ladies and gentlemen, will address the Convention.*

* This call was published in the *Seneca County Courier*, July 14, 1848, without any signatures. The movers of this Convention, who drafted

TO TELL PEOPLE ABOUT THE CONVENTION, THE WOMEN PLACED AN ANNOUNCEMENT IN THE LOCAL NEWSPAPER. THIS IS WHAT THE ANNOUNCEMENT SAID.

A GATHERING TO SUPPORT WOMEN

Because there were only a few days between the newspaper announcement and the beginning of the convention, a large crowd wasn't expected. But about 300 people attended—including 40 men!

Since the convention was about women and their rights, it was decided that men wouldn't be allowed to speak on the first day. However, on the second day, men were welcome to take part in the **discussions**. And the main discussion had to do with the statement prepared by Stanton.

KNOW THE FACTS!

ONE OF THE FAMOUS PEOPLE AT THE CONVENTION WAS FREDERICK DOUGLASS, A WELL-KNOWN SUPPORTER OF ABOLITION. HE HAD BEEN BORN INTO ENSLAVEMENT BUT ESCAPED AND LATER BOUGHT HIS FREEDOM.

STRANGELY ENOUGH, NONE OF THE WOMEN FELT COMFORTABLE LEADING THE CONVENTION. SO THEY ASKED LUCRETIA MOTT'S HUSBAND JAMES TO DO IT!

A DECLARATION OF WOMEN'S RIGHTS

Stanton prepared a declaration, or statement, of women's rights to be discussed at the convention. It was titled the Declaration of Sentiments.

Stanton based her declaration on the **Declaration of Independence**. It includes a listing of the unfair ways men have treated women. She also prepared a set of **resolutions** that listed the rights women could justly claim. The convention voted to approve, or authorize, the Declaration of Sentiments and resolutions. Then 100 people signed the Declaration—68 women and 32 men.

THIS CHART COMPARES PARTS OF THE DECLARATION OF SENTIMENTS AND THE DECLARATION OF INDEPENDENCE TO SHOW HOW STANTON BORROWED FROM THE EARLIER WRITING.

DECLARATION OF SENTIMENTS	DECLARATION OF INDEPENDENCE
We hold these truths to be self-evident; that all men and women are created equal	We hold these truths to be self-evident, that all men are created equal
Whenever any form of Government becomes **destructive** of these ends, it is the right of those who suffer from it to refuse **allegiance** to it, and to insist upon the institution of a new government	That whenever any Form of Government becomes destructive of these ends, it is the Right of the People to alter or to abolish it, and to institute a new Government
The history of mankind is a history of repeated injuries . . . on the part of man toward woman, having in direct object the establishment of an absolute **tyranny** over her	The history of the present King of Great Britain is a history of repeated injuries . . . all having in direct object the establishment of an absolute Tyranny over these States

KNOW THE FACTS!

THE RESOLUTION SUPPORTING WOMEN'S SUFFRAGE, OR THE RIGHT TO VOTE, SHOCKED MANY PEOPLE—INCLUDING LUCRETIA MOTT! FREDERICK DOUGLASS HELPED GET IT APPROVED BY SPEAKING IN FAVOR OF IT.

AFTER SENECA FALLS

Some newspapers made fun of the Seneca Falls Convention. But supporters of women's rights continued to fight for them.

Just 12 days after the Seneca Falls Convention, another meeting was held in Rochester, New York. A convention was held in Akron, Ohio, in 1851. Then, Stanton, Douglas, and Susan B. Anthony founded the American Equal Rights Association in 1866. Stanton and Anthony founded the National Woman Suffrage Association in 1869. But it wasn't until 1920 that women received the right to vote!

KNOW THE FACTS!

THE FIGHT FOR WOMEN'S RIGHTS DIDN'T END WHEN WOMEN RECEIVED THE RIGHT TO VOTE. WOMEN CONTINUED TO FIGHT FOR EQUAL TREATMENT IN EDUCATION, JOBS, AND SPORTS.

THESE ARE JUST SOME OF THE IMPORTANT EVENTS IN THE HISTORY OF WOMEN'S RIGHTS.

1848	CONVENTIONS IN SENECA FALLS AND ROCHESTER, NEW YORK
1851	CONVENTION IN AKRON, OHIO
1866	AMERICAN EQUAL RIGHTS ASSOCIATION FOUNDED
1869	NATIONAL WOMAN SUFFRAGE ASSOCIATION FOUNDED
1920	WOMEN RECEIVE THE RIGHT TO VOTE
1963	EQUAL PAY ACT IS PASSED, SAYING WOMEN AND MEN MUST BE PAID EQUALLY
1964	CIVIL RIGHTS ACT SAYS BOSSES CAN'T TREAT WOMEN DIFFERENTLY JUST BECAUSE THEY'RE WOMEN
1972	NEW LAW SAYS WOMEN MUST BE TREATED EQUALLY IN EDUCATION
2021	KAMALA HARRIS BECOMES FIRST WOMAN TO BE VICE PRESIDENT

SENECA FALLS TODAY

In 1980, the Women's Rights National Historical Park was established in Seneca Falls to honor the events that took place in 1848. It includes the Wesleyan Chapel where the convention met and Elizabeth Cady Stanton's home. It also includes the home of Mary Ann McClintock, where Stanton wrote the Declaration.

Over 1 million people have visited the park since it opened. You can visit too and learn more about the important events that happened there!

THIS WAS ELIZABETH CADY STANTON'S HOME. IT'S OPEN TO VISITORS TO THE WOMEN'S RIGHTS NATIONAL HISTORICAL PARK.

KNOW THE FACTS!

THE PARK ALSO INCLUDES THE HOME OF JANE HUNT, WHERE STANTON, MOTT, AND THE OTHER WOMEN MET FOR TEA AND PLANNED THE CONVENTION.

GLOSSARY

allegiance: Loyalty to one's country or leader.

anti-slavery: Against the practice of owning enslaved people.

Declaration of Independence: The piece of writing in which the colonies said they were free from British rule.

delegate: Someone who is chosen to vote or act for others.

destructive: Causing a great amount of harm.

discussion: The act of talking about something with others.

lawyer: Someone whose job it is to help people with their questions and problems with the law.

minister: A person who leads a church service.

resolution: An official statement of purpose voted on by a group.

self-evident: Clearly true and needing no proof.

support: To hold up or help a cause.

tyranny: Cruel and unfair treatment by people with power over others.

FOR MORE INFORMATION

Books

Olson, Gillia M. *The Life of Elizabeth Cady Stanton.* Mankato, MN: Amicus, 2022.

Orr, Tamra. *Susan B. Anthony's Women's Right to Suffrage Speech.* Ann Arbor, MI: Cherry Lake Publishing, 2021.

Websites

Lucretia Mott
www.dkfindout.com/us/history/womens-suffrage-in-america/lucretia-mott/
Read about this important organizer of the Seneca Falls Convention on this site.

Seneca Falls Convention: For Women, By Women
https://academy4sc.org/video/seneca-falls-convention-for-women-by-women/
Watch a video and read more about the Seneca Falls Convention on this website.

Publisher's note to educators and parents: Our editors have carefully reviewed these websites to ensure that they are suitable for students. Many websites change frequently, however, and we cannot guarantee that a site's future contents will continue to meet our high standards of quality and educational value. Be advised that students should be closely supervised whenever they access the internet.

INDEX